Facing The Music

By

Curtis "Caliber" Vanzant Jr

FACING THE MUSIC

Copyright © 2015 by Curtis "Caliber" Vanzant Jr. All rights reserved. Printed in the United States of America. No part of this publication may be used, reproduced, transmitted and or broadcasted in any form by any means without written permission from publishing author. Except for brief quotations embodied in critical articles and reviews. Spoken at events may be accepted acknowledging the author. This book can be purchased for educational use for appropriate portions thereof, business or sales promotional use. This is a work of fiction. Names, characters, places, and incidents either are the product of the author's imagination or are used fictitiously, any resemblance to actual persons, living or dead, business establishments, events, or locales is entirely coincidental.

For more information or written permission please address by email ccaliberdapoet@gmail.com

Library of Congress Cataloging-in-Publication Data

Vanzant, Curtis, 1982-

Facing The Music

ISBN- 13: 978-0692462058

ISBN- 10: 0692462058

Facing The Music

By

Curtis "Caliber" Vanzant Jr

Caliber Van Publishing

Contents

Introduction 7

Scene One 9

Scene Two 13

Scene Three 19

Scene Four 29

Scene Five 35

Scene Six 41

Scene Seven 47

Scene Eight 51

Scene Nine 59

Scene Ten 69

Scene Eleven 75

Scene Twelve 81

Scene Thirteen 89

Scene Fourteen 95

Scene Fifteen 99

Characters

Jason..Old friend

Ebony..Girlfriend

Paris..Sister

Anthony...Ebony's Son

Tizz..An Associate

Fan 1..Female

Fan 2..Male

Germane..A Host

Water...The Poetess

Dude..A Problem

Co-Workers...Company

Officer...The Law

Introduction

There comes a time. In a particular situation when a bad or near death experience is realer than you can ever imagine. Oblivious at first to how powerful words can create tension or even come true. Once it hits the fan you are now facing the music.

Growing up, my mom told me when I was a kid I wanted to be the guy working at the gas station providing services for the customers to pump their gas. At the time she told me that, I thought wow, I just remember wanting to be a pediatrician doctor as an adolescent. However, I never pursued that. I don't know if God had other plans for me or what. I always loved all the arts, such as martial arts, sketches, paintings etc. I even used to draw gym shoes back in the day. Somehow my focus and interest changed slightly with poetry. Not for once did I think of how big and well known I would become in this, it was just something that I was more consistent with. I assume that counts the most in anything a person does. I also have not seen anybody rich doing what I do, but they definitely make an impact in people's lives. Behind what the audience and fans see, there are many challenges such as trial and error. I stay strong throughout them all in what I write. These few months were different. Realizing that there is an advantage and disadvantage to everything. I also thought what if stop performing and just continued to work. None of these incidents would have ever happened. By the way, they call me "Apache," from Indiana, and this is my story, a poet's story.

~Scene One~

The music plays from cd in his car, "Recycled Souls." While driving he gets a text message from a friend that he ignores for now. The friend calls him and he answers.

Apache: "What up J what's going on."

Jason: "I just called to see if you were available for my first show."

Apache: "What………first show!" [Laughing]

Jason: "I'm serious."

Apache: "Congratulations man. I didn't know if you were gonna stick with poetry or just keep doing what you do."

Jason: "Naw, I'm just on disability from injuring my back so I can't do much."

Apache: "Damn, sorry to hear that bro."

Jason: "Yeah, it's cool. I just want to put together a show. No heavy lifting but I still got mouths to feed you know."

Apache: "I know that's right."

Jason: "I will text you all the info later, but this is two months in advance April 19th on a Saturday."

Apache: "Oh ok during National Poetry Month that's wassup."

Jason: "Yeah, we gonna get up way before that though."

Apache: "Ok just hit my line."

We hang up the phone as I turn into my driveway to walk in. I never thought of coming home to a woman and still not happy. I just deal with it for now because I don't have the extra time and I don't feel like dating. Since I don't have any kids and she doesn't want anymore because of the unbearable labor pains that she had with her only son, we have our differences. We get along but sometimes we don't. Her son Anthony and I like bowling and going out for pizza. Many times we do those things without her now and he is 12 years old. Meanwhile, my focus has been based on my 9 to 5 to keep paying these bills and spoken word on the side while I'm ahead. That's less stressful. I open the door and she greets me with a hug and kiss.

~Scene Two~

Ebony: "Hey baby, how was your day? I cooked."

Apache: "It was cool. I will eat later I need to get some stuff done first."

Ebony: "Ok"

After hours goes by I eat what my baby cooked. Which was fried chicken, mashed potatoes with gravy, and steamed broccoli with cheese. She sits with me while I eat.

Apache: "You wanna know something that is all so true?"

Ebony: "What?"

Apache: "This food is delicious."

Ebony: "Well of course because I cooked it." [Laughing]

Apache: "So what are you trying to say, I can't cook?"

Ebony: "No I'm not saying that baby, you know I will eat what you cook when you do every twice a month." [Laughing]

Apache: "Umm ok. You just hurt my masculine feelings with that."

Ebony: "Awe, but you have other qualities that I like and more that you make up for though."

Apache: "Oh really, now what will one of them be?"

Ebony: "I rather show you but my son still doing his homework."

Apache: "Well once I get done with this second plate I will go check on him ok. Meanwhile you get ready for your presentation." [Laughing]

Ebony: "Yes" [Laughing]

The next day I go to work. What is my occupation? Well, I work for a marketing company that helps businesses in developing marketing strategies for organizations. That involves some troubleshooting if needed. I identify the S.W.O.T and create marketing plans for them to implement if they like. In which they do, especially when it comes from me. What do I consider an accomplishment? I have my own office and been recommended over fifty times to write plans outlined in simple documents for other companies. Been doing this for three years for them, but created my own portfolio from doing the same thing for small businesses as a marketing consultant for hire after college with a Bachelor's degree in Marketing Management. I learned that this is more important to them, than it was to me at the time and I get paid well to do it now. I rather get a salary pay instead of commission. In so many words, I get paid to tell and show you in detail on how you should run your own business effectively from a demographic stand point to achieve that success that you reach for to meet demands and organizational goals. Sounds easy, but not quite, you must read their mission statement. To find out the scope and to understand what it is that they really want to do and how they want to go about getting there.

Curtis Caliber Vanzant Jr

~Scene Three~

Curtis Caliber Vanzant Jr

Open mic tonight at an old spot I haven't been to in at least seven months. Good to see they still got it going on hosted by an associate named Tizz. We had a disagreement that was understood later and forgiven. It was a time that I came to his spot once before to promote a show that I was featuring in. Which was ok, but he had something going on, on that same date. I had no idea. We both can get people to come out to events that we are in and really it's up to that person to come up with that decision on what event they want to go to. That confused me about the situation. Like I said it was understood later and we are cool, no grudges held. Besides that, I hosted an open mic back at home and again out here in Houston on Thursdays nights for one year in the past called, "Spit on It," that he did come out to support. We shook hands.

Tizz: "Say it ain't so, what up Apache. How you been?"

Apache: "I'm good."

Tizz: "Ok, well you know you can always spit here if you want, thanks for coming."

Apache: "Yeah nice crowd I see."

Tizz: "Hell yeah, I got some amazing talent lined up, I will call you up in a minute if you ready."

Apache: "I been ready ever since I graduated high school fool." [Laughing]

Tizz: [Laughing]

Time passes with good vibes and beautiful people on top of the talent I am witnessing. After listening to a few singers and poets, he calls me up.

Tizz: "I hope yawl ready for some more. If you not I suggest you get ready. Most of us know this brother already for how he gets down when he do what he does when he does it on the mic. He has hosted shows before, a two time author, and a slam winner. So stand up and give him a warm welcome back, for APACHE!!!!!

Apache: "Give it up for Tizz too. As long as I have known this dude, he always got something going on. I really appreciate all the love that yawl been giving me out here too. Anyway, I got something short and to the point to recite."

Who Am I

"They call me Apache

From Indiana

Been doing this shit for years

While behind these scenes

My pen bleeds

The blood, sweat, and tears

Profusely

Creating

Masterpieces sporadically

But I was born for this

And this spoken word

Don't make you rich

I'm that

Same dude

That graduated

From that

First black high school

Even after

I get my taxes

Still trying to balance

My career with what

I love

They say follow your heart

But my mind knows better

Instead of

Chasing cheddar

And sex

I confess

When it comes to me

I'm just not

Down for whatever

A selective desire

If I was to get

Facing The Music

Arthritis in my right hand

I would learn

How to write

With my left

The pieces

That I wrote

That you like

The most

Is when shit

Went left

But I'm like

A locomotive with no brakes

Keeping it moving

Through down falls

And heartbreaks

Because whatever it is

Positive

> That you are pursuing
>
> It shall happen
>
> As long as you
>
> Pray for it too"

[Clapping, standing ovation, phones out, flashing lights]

Tizz: "Give it up more time for Apache yawl!"

We shake hands and he whispers in my ear.

Tizz: "Apache stay for a little bit, I wanna talk to you about something."

Apache: "Ok"

Ebony calls as he walks off stage.

Apache: "Hey what's up."

Ebony: "Where you at?"

Apache: "I just thought to stop by this open mic real quick after work."

Ebony: "But you didn't think to stop and call me right."

Apache: "Look don't start. I will be home in a minute. What you doing?"

Ebony: "Nothing playing board games with Anthony."

Apache: "Well I will be home shortly."

People start to leave as the show comes to an end.

Fan 1: "I just wanted to say I enjoyed what you said tonight. Do you have a card or are you on social media or something?"

Apache: "Yea sure. You can find me on Time book and Me tube."

Fan 1: "Ok thanks. Are you coming back to this spot next time?"

Apache: "I don't know I just might."

Fan 2: "Dude that was a nice piece I gotta admit. I'm author."

Apache: "Thanks. You went up too?"

Fan 2: "Yeah just before you walked in. I respect what you said though. I will look you up."

Apache: "Ok cool"

Tizz: "Apache man I appreciate you for coming out. What you think about featuring for next Thursday?"

Apache: "Yeah that's cool."

Tizz: "I know I can give you at least $200 if that's cool."

Apache: "Yeah that's cool. I will be back. I gotta go."

Tizz: "Ok take care."

Apache: "You too bro."

~Scene Four~

Curtis Caliber Vanzant Jr

After all that is said and done, it was just after midnight and I'm exhausted. Not to mention I have to be at work by 9 a.m. I need my rest and I'm going to get it. My girl and her son is sleep. I really don't do this as often as I use to, but it's good to get out sometimes expressing myself. Just been writing, working, and dealing with life really. I haven't performed in over six months. I have a meeting around noon with a potential client later today to negotiate a marketing plan. I should be getting an email with their attached mission statement this morning before noon so I can have these documents ready by noon.

If there is one thing that I know that I need to stop doing, it would be drinking coffee. I honestly don't think it has nothing to do with keeping you up. I also think it's true about caffeine being unhealthy, and one cup can be four trips to the restroom within the first thirty minutes. I don't do energy drinks. I may look healthy probably because I'm not obese, but I need to eat healthy too. I love me some soul food. Plus I'm allergic to some seafood but can eat shrimp that is high in potassium too. The weekend is finally here and now I'm off for two days that just feels to me like one. Once I get these documents sent off to clients, I will be done.

I like to say that this is when my day actually begins. Anthony's birthday is approaching and I was thinking of getting him something. One of my friends ask me one day, he said, "Man why you care about that little boy so much? He is not even yours." I replied, "I might not be the best with kids and who is, even for the ones that do have kids. But the kid reminds me of my little brother Darius." He was killed at a house party over the weekend after a fight broke out. He wasn't even the one fighting. What happen to the shooter? The hell if I know because nobody there wanted to talk to the police or even came forwarded afterwards. All those people there and they just heard gunshots. Apparently they supposed to be his friends or he wouldn't felt comfortable enough to go in the first place. As far as I'm concerned, nobody from that party shouldn't have came to his funeral, just family and people that wasn't there when he got killed that night. That's how I fell. It made the news and I still keep the paper to this day. He was a smart kid that died at the age of 17 years old. The case still remains unsolved. Violence is everywhere and for some folks it's not so much of a concern for them until it hits home. That's when it becomes a personal matter. So when it did, I moved to Chicago.

The move to Chicago was a little convenient for me because of the commute time between home and work. A lot goes on out there and I definitely didn't escape violence either. This city is actually one of the five locations that the company has. Which are Indianapolis, IN, Chicago, IL, Alpharetta, GA, Greensboro, NC, and Houston, TX. The windy city is very big on poetry among other things and diverse. Seems like every weekend something is going on. I even participated in a few poetry slams and enjoyed the night life of some venues and clubs downtown. It was cool, but I moved again two years later. My sister Paris lives in Indianapolis. I go there from time to time to visit my nieces and nephews as well as friends and colleagues. No matter where I go I always look to spit somewhere. It's a lot easier now that I am well known in some places. I used to tell my sister I want to move there, so I can be closer to them, but instead I moved all the way south to Houston, TX. That was when I met Ebony and started courting her. She was raised by her grandparents at first because her parents died in a car accident when she was just two years old. They strapped her in a car seat, but didn't put their seatbelts on. At the age of ten her grandfather died of prostate cancer. Her child's father dealt drugs, in what we refer to as a dope boy, and is serving federal time in prison. After me and her dated for a year I decided that she and her son stay with me. A lot of nights I came home to myself. So I thought it was a good idea.

~Scene Five~

Curtis Caliber Vanzant Jr

Little Anthony sits with me as I read the paper at the kitchen table as if he was bored.

Anthony: "I see old people that read the paper a lot. Why you read the paper you not that old?"

[Laughing] Apache: "I have to keep up with the current events."

Anthony: "Why people don't call you Jeremy?"

Apache: "Well because most people here only know me as an artist."

Anthony: "You know how to draw?"

[Laughing] Apache: "No and it's not that type of art. Why you asking so many questions huh? Do you have homework?"

Anthony: "No"

Apache: "Are you sure?"

Anthony: "Yup"

Apache: "Ok because I am smarter than a six grader so I can help you ok."

Anthony: "Ok"

Apache: "So did you think about what you want to do for your birthday?"

Anthony: "I want to go to that place where they got the arcades and go carts at. And I want to go, and I want to go with you to see you do poetry."

Apache: "Oh really." [Laughing]

Apache: "Well we can do the arcade thing, but I will have to see if there is a place that is doing poetry on that night ok."

Anthony: "Ok"

Apache: "When is your birthday tomorrow right?"

Anthony: [Nod's head yes]

Apache: "In the meantime, I have a little assignment for you since you don't have homework. It's not much though. I want you to look up these three words that I like to call the 3c's. (Caesura, Couplet and Connotation) I want you to write down the definition and give an example of each ok."

Anthony: "Ok"

Apache: "You have a curious mind so that should be fun for you. So go do that so I can see it later."

As Anthony leaves the kitchen to go to his room, here comes Ebony with her jacket on to grab her keys to her car.

Apache: "Where you going?"

Ebony: "It's Friday, ladies night."

Apache: "Alright then………..Anthony said he wants to go to Birthday City for his birthday."

Ebony: "Damn, I knew something was coming up. I just couldn't think of what it was. I won't be able to make that."

Apache: "What!!"

Apache: "What the hell you gotta do that's more important than your son's birthday?"

Ebony: "Jeremy stay out my business! You don't see me asking about yours!"

Apache: "Wow….ok. I guess I suppose to just, come up with my own story on why you not coming huh!"

[Door slams]

~Scene Six~

Curtis Caliber Vanzant Jr

Facing The Music

I make calls and texting to find out is there an open mic going on for that night. Not even anything on my page right now of any. Later on, a friend of mine came through for me with a text about a spot on the other side of town but not far from where we are going. Little man and I are having a ball. One thing I can say is that you can never stop liking go carts no matter how old you get. Anthony got his hands on a fast one too. I was right behind him with mines. Other people were no match for us. I got him all the tokens for the arcades and pizza he wanted. We sat down for a minute is when he asked me. Is my mom coming? I didn't want to lie to him so I told him the truth. No she is not coming. He puts his head down for a minute. I can tell he was sad, but didn't cry. The night is not over yet. Plus he impressed me at the house with that little homework assignment I gave to him. I'm really tired now, but it's time to take him to this open mic with me. I can't just spectate; he wants to see me perform. So I write my name on the list, I'm number four. As time passes he looks like he is enjoying himself. This one female poet did catch my attention though with what she was saying. She was nice with it and kind of cute too. I felt like a groupie for like five seconds to be honest. I had to remain professional. Let's just say after she spoke I became an instant fan.

Germane: "Coming to the stage next, this brother has put in a lot of work from shows, to slams, to books. And the energy you give is what he will give back. So show this brother some love because he is no amateur to this. Apache!!

Apache performs "Who Am I" (Clean version)

Germane informs me that his spot is new. And if I can come back letting people know to come, that we definitely can talk business. I rather get back to him on that because I have some other personal things going on right now. I can't be at two places at once considering time and distance. Plus, I have no idea what is going on with Ebony. After the open mic on our way back home I asked Anthony, did he enjoy himself? He replied, yes he did. As a matter of fact he said he would like to go again. Then he asked me to give him some more words to look up to know. Once we get back to the house Ebony is still not there and it's 12:47a.m. I write down four words this time for him. (Emphasis, Aphorism, Epiphany, Euphony)

Ebony walks in almost two hours later intoxicated. Majority of the time my assumptions be right on, so I don't mind being an ass. Call it a man's intuition. They sleep while I prepare a few things for two presentations for Monday. I have been doing my job and nothing extra but I heard a rumor that I was up for employee of the month and promotion. This was great if you can look at the big picture. I get a call from Jason about the upcoming show. We schedule to meet and hang out to talk at a lounge after I get off work.

Curtis Caliber Vanzant Jr

~Scene Seven~

Curtis Caliber Vanzant Jr

Jason: "What up Apache"

Apache: "Nothing much man just maintaining."

Jason: "So you know we like a month and a half away from April 19th."

Apache: "Yeah I know."

Jason: "This show is gonna be big, I can feel it boss. I made some flyers and put your face on it since you are the feature if that's cool with you."

Apache: "Yeah sure that's cool."

Apache: "Where you able to sell tickets yet?"

Jason: "A few. You can take some too."

Apache: "Normally I would but honestly I got some personal shit going on. I can take some flyers though."

Jason: "Ok well here goes a few. Just do what you can, I understand. I got more people in the show that can sell some too."

Jason: "I totally understand though. Some people only see what they see on stage, not knowing what it took or that feeling that you didn't ask for that got those words out."

Apache: "Right"

Jason: "It's almost like facing the music sort of speak."

Apache: "Exactly"

~Scene Eight~

That night came to an end. I needed my rest for work the next day. As for work, it went by smoothly. My parent's anniversary is in two weeks. They have been married for thirty-seven years. That is a long time I must say. I don't know anyone from my generation that can even do seven and for the right reasons to be married. I wanted to celebrate with them so I booked a roundtrip Midwest Airline ticket to come. I got time to take off so why not use some of it for that. I am fortunate to still have them around. I check on them every now and then. Ebony has keys to my house for her and Anthony. I would have asked if they wanted to come but Anthony has school. Ebony met my parents before but the way things are going, I think not.

The time is now for that trip to visit my parents. I'm excited to come back to my hometown because it's been a long time. I even get to see my sister again all in one trip. If my little brother was alive he would be twenty-four years old. Sometimes I wonder what he would have been doing or trying to pursue at that age. Happy to see me, my parents welcomes me with open arms and I spend the day with them. My sister drives and comes later that day. We all go to dinner and toast to their Thirty-seventh anniversary.

Apache: "Congratulations mom and dad and many more to come!"

Paris: "Yes and many more indeed."

The next day I checked my page to see what is going on tonight. An old friend told me about a spot in which I really don't mind going to because it's in my hometown Gary, IN. I see the host is still doing her thing with a new venue this time. I leave the stage like I do every stage now, I rip it apart. Sometimes I think that my poetry is more meaningful than my career. So I continue to speak to the people to inspire, entertain, and most of all to remain strong throughout obstacles that we may come cross. I call my house and no one answers. I call Ebony's grandmother's house. She tells me Ebony dropped her son off about an hour ago. I notified her that I will be back Thursday. Meanwhile a friend of mine wants me to pick him up to go to this comedy club. I admit I need a laugh. I pick him up and we go to the event. This place is packed and all I really came for is a couple of drinks and some jokes. The host acknowledges me, telling everyone to give me a round of applause as I walked in. I really wasn't looking to be noticed for what I do, just coming out to unwind. My friend and I get to the bar to order food and drinks. These comedians are hilarious. I just don't like sometimes that knowing my city is run down and needs work, instead of using their material they would talk about my city badly as a joke as if they were trying to be facetious. The total opposite in the jokes they would tell in a major more beautiful city like Miami for instance. Maybe it's just me being sensitive is what some may call it. Unfortunately, that night was cut short because I have to catch my flight in the morning.

Back in Houston and back to work until the weekend again. Ebony says that she wants to move out. I actually came home to her packing her belongings. I told her, whoever this dude is you might as well move out because you spend a lot of time with him than you do for your own son and me. I was curious to know and she told me the truth finally. That she has been seeing this dude either while I'm at work or at an open mic. I'm assuming when I went out of town she was thrilled. I even confronted her about what her grandmother told me when I called from out of town. Her grandmother said verbatim, "You know Ebony pregnant." Ebony admits that it is true for two weeks now. And it's not mine. So yeah, I think it's best to give me my keys and leave. Anthony is sad but hopefully I can still see him. He says he is sorry, but it's not his fault at all.

    I still hang out from time to time but when I return home it's just me again alone. I have been focusing on these new clients for the past two weeks. Anthony wants to go bowling. I pick him up and we do just that. As I move around I pass out flyers and tell people about the April 19th show coming up. The next day off work I stop at a gas station. While pumping my gas this dude drives up beside my car and approaches me. Ebony's alleged baby's father to unborn child. He claims that this is no threat, but that he seriously suggests that I stay away from Ebony and her son period. He then gets back in his car with somebody in the passenger seat and drives off. I shake my head thinking. Obviously she left me for this no good ass dude and I can careless on getting her back. I'm upset but refuse to leave a voicemail on her phone because she is not answering. The next day her grandmother asked me to pick up Anthony from school because he doesn't have a ride home. Usually he gets dropped off to her house from one of his friend's parents. I agree to pick him up and drop him off. I told him that we won't spend as much time together as we would like right now, but I will definitely be around if he needs me. I remember telling Jason I wasn't going to do too much promoting just passing out flyers, but I changed my mind. Dude been in my corner for years plus this is his first show. Not to mention that a lot will be going on that whole month regarding poetry for at least three days a week in different spots. I get an invite back to Germane's spot. It's Showtime!!

Curtis Caliber Vanzant Jr

~Scene Nine~

Curtis Caliber Vanzant Jr

Germane: "Thanks for coming back. I know I sent you an invite, but I was just about to call you to see if you would come out again. We got a much bigger crowd than before."

Apache: "Yeah I see."

Germane: "When do you want to go up?"

Apache: "It don't matter, just not last and not first. Number seven is cool."

Germane: "I think you was number four last time but ok cool seven."

I try to relax and clear my head with the crap I'm dealing with before I go up. Not always effective, but over the course of nineteen years I have learned that. It will be moments where you will have no time to prepare so instead you improvise. As talented people goes on and off the stage I drink my long island at the bar and wait. A few people came up to take pictures. I even sold a few tickets to the show and one copy of my book.

Water: "So you decided to come back huh."

Apache: "Hey, you look familiar from the last time I was here."

Water: "I liked that piece you recited last time."

Apache: "Thanks I appreciate that coming from you because you were pretty good yourself. What is your name again?"

Water: "My name is Water."

Apache: "Nice to meet you again."

Apache: "I remember you saying something last time like, "to just add water." You had the audience rolling on that part." [Laughing]

Water: "Yeah" [Laughing]

Water: "Was that your son you were with last time?"

Apache: "No but it's a long story."

Water: "Well sorry if I was being nosy I just thought to ask."

Apache: "Naw it's cool."

Germane: "You will be going up after her ok."

Apache: "Ok"

The poetess that goes by the name "Water" performs her piece.

What Leaks

"What leaks is the truth

No virgin to mic

So I'm not exactly pure

But for damn sure

Not contaminated

While some be left

Fascinated

I can careless

On what you can do with it

Just let it be

Because if you not

My cup of tea

Than how you

Gonna hold it

Down for me as my King

No offense but for starters

A man is not complete

Unless

He finds his Queen

So just add water

I'm what you need

But still taken for granted

Like one of the three

Necessities

Boy please

I'm tired

Nor am I

Looking for another Samson

To seduce

Because I'm far

From a prostitute like Delilah

Just call me

The modern day female messiah

Not for hire

Let my pieces be

The tissues for your tears

On whatever it is

You going through

To move forward

With no fears

And to understand life

As we

See it

Today"

Apache performs his piece.

Poetry History

"Many young folks

Have used the term

Turn up

So turn it up

For words like this

Especially published

In books

For they speak volumes

Make room

Great minds

Of great ones in history

You now have

More company

Regarding poetry

I'm not always

As serene

As one may think

But it just might

Capture the ambience

That helps an individual be

Resilient under conditions

Of stress

In which kills"

Curtis Caliber Vanzant Jr

~Scene Ten~

After the open mic they talked a little more. Since they were both starving they met up at a nice elegant restaurant to eat where they had someone playing the piano.

Apache: "Table for two please."

Apache: "So Water, what is your real name if you don't mind me asking?"

Water: "Kendra, which means water baby, along with other meanings."

Apache: "Well nice to properly meet you, I'm Jeremy, which means Jeremy."

Water: "Oh that's funny." [Laughing]

Apache: "To be honest I wasn't trying to ask you out on a date. I was just hungry and don't mind being spontaneous. Thought maybe you was a starving artist too."

Water: [Laughing] "Yeah I was. I usually eat before an open mic but I didn't this time, trying to watch my weight."

Apache: "Yeah, yeah, yeah" [Laughing]

Apache: "So what inspires you to write?"

Water: "Life"

Apache: "Just one word huh."

Water: "Yeah, because water is essential to life. Just like the woman I am, essential."

Apache: "Oh ok true and interesting. What do you do for a living?"

Apache: "Are you from here?"

Water: "No Beaumont, TX. As far as my career goes I am a nurse at the hospital."

Water: "I have three questions for you. How long have you been living here in H-town and what made you move?" It's something about you. You like a different type of caliber."

Apache: "Maybe because I'm not from here I don't know. If everybody was the same then the world would be boring instead of interesting. It's cool to have some things in common though."

Water: "True"

Apache: "I have been living here for five years now. I moved to start over and I'm 34 years old, just in case you ask me that." [Laughing]

Water: [Laughing] "Ok since you want to be one step ahead which is fine with me. What are my next questions? By the way, I'm 32."

Apache: "Umm…..I have no idea what those next questions are."

Water: [Laughing] "What do you do for a living besides poetry and are you single?"

Apache: "I am a marketing associate for a company." [Pause]

Water: "Ok that's cool. I guess I should ask that question again. Are you single?"

Apache: "Yes I am very much so. However my situation is still complicated and I rather not get into it right now."

Water: "Ok cool I can somewhat understand that. I know that it has been a long time since I had pasta though. And I never been to this restaurant."

Apache: "Yeah me neither but it was close plus I love Italian food."

We continue to talk more as the waitress take our plates, but still drinking on our glasses of red wine. I really wanted to tell her my situation but rather elaborate on that some other time. Eventually we ended up calling it a night and going our separate ways. I did ask for her number just to keep in touch. She refused to give it to me in which made me laugh. She said that she was sure we will meet again even if we didn't plan to. I agreed and finally went home to get some sleep. Work as usual, I get a call from the hospital and it's Anthony. His mom is in the hospital beat up. I go to the hospital to see her. She was sleep but didn't look too good. The doctor said that she had some mild head trauma but will recover. She needs her rest. Meanwhile, Anthony says that he wants to stay at my house for tonight instead of going to his GGma's house. That's what he likes to call her. I will just take him to school in the morning and drop him off afterwards. Anthony told me what has been going on with his mom that didn't sound nice at all.

[Fast Forward]……………

~Scene Eleven~

Facing The Music

I dropped Anthony off from school. I drive off. By the time I get to the second stop sign, it's him again, the alleged father to unborn child. Pulling up on the side of me. With the audacity, to demand for me to pull over. Ok cool.

Apache: "Look dude I'm about tired of you and you not even the police, you pull over."

Dude: "Ok"

He runs up on me quick and I give him a quick kick to the knee, he buckles falling forward, and a jab to the face. Once he falls, I take his gun out his waist and take the magazine out. Take the gun apart, and then hit him three more times in the face to see blood.

Apache: "Look man, I'm not crazy but apparently you are because you don't know me. Plus I don't care to know you. From the looks of it I got more shit to lose than you do. So I strongly seriously suggest you stay the hell away from me! I don't want Ebony, but you need to stop beating on her I know that!"

One last punch to his face and I walk to my car and drive off with his clip in my pocket. I don't need it but neither does he. Guns are only dangerous as the person behind it. Even being in the wrong hands of adolescences, the word "protection," is overrated. So I went to a gas station and threw away the clip in the garbage, and the bullets in another. I need to focus back on work. It's a shame that all this is happening.

    I go home to take in all of this. I take a deep breath, lie on my bed and just stare at the ceiling in complete silence until I fall asleep. Thinking of what could I have possibly done wrong that led up to this and how can I stop it without violence. It seems like for some folks that is the only thing they understand. Over nonsense if you ask me. I don't bark loud and have learned that any emotions, feelings, and or thoughts should be written down. It can be profitable and can mean more let alone help someone else. Karma has been paid me back with interest already. From lost loved ones, jail time, to heart break. I have never taken a life and don't plan to, but have starred down the barrel of a gun before that actually did scare me. From that point on I looked in the mirror and told myself. I will fear no one or nothing but God. Why should I when we all have to leave this world someday. The objective is to make the most of it in a positive way and to touch others along the way.

Back to work, I got some documents to print out and a presentation with the team for some clients. I almost forgot about tonight. The company is having a bowling night. I can't wait to show them a little thing or two. Maybe it will get me to relax and get my mind of that bullshit. I invited Water through social media to see if she would like to come. She said yes once she get done with her shift she would.

~Scene Twelve~

Apache: "Co-workers this Kendra. Kendra these are some of the people I work with."

Co-workers: "Hi Kendra"

We are having a good time plus I'm doing better than expected. It looks like she knows how to bowl too. We bowl three games with my co-workers. They left after that, we stayed a little longer and walked to the bar they have there.

Water: "So you never told me what inspires you or how you came up with your name?"

Apache: "A lot inspires me even people. Apache was just a name I came up with. People started to add the Indiana part to it once I moved from the state."

Water: "So poetry is not the only thing you good at I see. You can bowl too."

Apache: "I do alright."

Water: "Modest too huh"

Apache: [Laughing] "I see you rolling them strikes out there."

Water: "Yeah I use to be in tournaments I lost my touch." [Laughing]

Apache: "Oh is that right, ok." [Laughing]

Water: "So are you ready for your big show April 19th? The flyers are everywhere; I even heard about it on the radio."

Apache: "Yeah I'm ready. Are you coming?"

Water: "Of course I'm coming. I wouldn't miss it for the world."

Water: "How is that situation coming along?"

Apache: "What situation?"

Water: "You know the one that you don't want to tell me."

Apache: "I'm trying to handle it."

Water: "Why you just can't tell me?"

Apache: "I don't want to alarm you or for it to be like a red flag or something."

Water: "Well just so you know. I don't like secrets."

Apache: "I'm sure you don't and neither do I. It's not all that bad on my part anyway."

Water: "You need to tell me soon I know that much if we decide to go further."

Apache: "Ok"

She thought it was at least ok for me to follow her home to make sure she made it safely. Not to mention she has no kids. Not saying that I would have thought different. I walked her to the door and she gives me her card. She tells me she had a good time. Reminding me of my situation I should tell her that doesn't really concern her. A kiss from her soft lips she gives me. Then I give her a real kiss and tell her to have a goodnight. I walked back to my car before I ended up telling her after that. I almost did after that kiss. The next day I get a call about an audition that I sent in months ago, to perform on national TV. I completely forgot about that audition. I'm scheduled to get on a plane to go to New York City, NY for four days. This was definitely a good opportunity to show the rest of the world my gift. I went out there and treated it like it wasn't a big show so I won't be as nervous and did my thing as usual.

I get back to Houston feeling good. Knowing that I just did something that means so much to me in front of the biggest audience I ever performed in front of. It was memorable I must say, and so for my people back home. My parents and sister Paris calls to say congratulations. No compensation just exposure. Paying for my flight and room was enough. The show I have to do with my guy Jason was also coming up real soon. He called me excited saying that I can bring a bigger crowd and that I should do an interview on the radio. He manages to get more air time to get people aware of April 19th, which is in one week. I didn't say a word about the show to co-workers and they already know. They just might come to.

A day before the show I get paranoid. I was weary about if we have enough security there. So I called Jason to see. He says that he got everything covered and to just show up and do me. I look at my phone. A text from Kendra, "I seen you on TV the other day congrats well done." I reply, "Thanks." I went to the police department to tell them that we need more security at the show to make sure everything goes good and as planned. They stated that they will send a few unmarked vehicles to the location for the entire show.

On the day of the show I stopped at the gas station to get gas.

Curtis Caliber Vanzant Jr

Facing The Music

~Scene Thirteen~

On my way I get pulled over by the police. He walks up to my car and asks for my license and registration. I give it to him along with my insurance card. The officer goes back to his squad car to check everything. Meanwhile, I'm in the car thinking, what he could possibly have on me. That's when it came to me, my gun permit. When I moved to Chicago then Houston I changed everything, but forgot to change my address on my gun permit. He comes back to my car.

Officer: "Do you have a gun in the car?"

Apache: "Yes I do."

Officer: "Where is it?"

Apache: "In my glove compartment officer."

He tells me to step out the car and frisk me and to stand by my trunk while he goes to the other side to get my gun.

Officer: "Do you have a permit for this?"

Apache: "Yes sir I do."

He checks and comes back 20 minutes later.

Officer: "I will have to confiscate this gun."

Apache: "Officer I was trying to get to a show that I suppose to be performing at. I am not looking for trouble."

Officer: "Look I can careless about a show. You have to follow the laws out here. Now I could take you to jail, but I'm not going to do that. I will have to take this gun."

Officer: "You can get it back when you get another gun permit with your current address on it. Plus training is required. You must complete a DPS authorized gun safety training course taught by a certified instructor. Go online or apply at the DPS office and they will tell you everything you need to know. Pay your fee, and the process should take up to 60 days after you completed training with a letter saying if it was rejected or approved."

Apache: "Ok"

Officer: "You have a good night."

Apache: "Yeah thanks"

Well thanks to the cop that was just doing his job. I don't have protection for myself now, knowing that I was just at the police station earlier. I'm sure he had no idea and doesn't know me, but this is messed up. I can imagine the cops outside the venue sitting in their cars just talking about sports or something and not paying attention. Anyway, I go over a few lines in one of my pieces before walking in. I get out and started to walk to the door. By the time I get close to the door a car pulls up with tinted windows and rolls down one. Somebody yelled out, "What's up chief!" I turn towards the car and several rounds fired at me go off while standing there. The one dude in passenger seat attempted to finish me off but seen the unmark police car making a U-turn with sirens. He quickly got back in the car and they took off as the police chase them down. One shot probably was the one that shattered the glass door and I was hit twice. The bouncer was hit in the abdomen; he was standing on the inside of that glass door. He died at the scene. The music stopped and people wanted to see what happened. Ladies came out screaming. The bouncer is dead and I'm right outside the entrance on the ground bleeding. I was rushed to the hospital. I woke up a day later in a room full of people including my parents, sister, people that was there and the police. The people that were not immediate family had to step out. The doctor was checking my vital signs when he asked me to nod my head if I can understand him. I nod yes and try to speak. He tells me not to. He also tells me that I was grazed in the neck that missed my cervical vertebrae. That could have done more damage. "You may have some minor neck spasms in life but you will be fine. You were shot in the right thigh and it didn't do any damage to any arteries or nerves. Both wounds were through and through. I dealt with cases like this and you are very lucky not to be paralyzed or dead. If the paramedics didn't come as fast as they did you probably would have bled to death." There were two men in that car and when they fled the scene it became a police pursuit. About a mile away they crashed. They survived and were taken into custody.

Facing The Music

~Scene Fourteen~

Curtis Caliber Vanzant Jr

Months later after healing, Jason comes by my house to check on me. I told him I apologize for what happened. He reminds me that it was not my fault that happened, but I know he lost some money for that. People performed and I was supposed to go last and never did. So just thinking about that part I gave him a thousand dollars in an envelope. He turns it down for a second and I insisted. He thanks me and tells me that he will host another event someday soon. I told him maybe I shouldn't be the headliner next time. He laughs as if that was a joke. I was serious. I informed him that I had a bad feeling that's why I asked about security due to all the promoting that was going on. I finally told Kendra everything and she understood. They gave both men 35 years with no possibility of parole each for attempted murder, murder, fleeing the scene, damaging property, and no permit to carry firearm. One of the dudes got out of prison a year and two months ago. Throughout all this, Kendra stayed by my side. Ebony apologized like four times to me and is attending college. Her son Anthony is doing just fine. I see him every now and then. Even on some occasions when me and Kendra go out. I constantly get calls about featuring in other states. I admit it is hard to turn down what I love. A university contacted me and wanted me to speak and perform and I did. I turned down a few offers until I got another one from my inbox on social media saying, "Would you like to make $1,200 to feature in Tampa FL?" Excluding the paid flight and room was cool. To feature with one of the biggest heavy hitting poet out there as well, I accepted. I only had to pay for Kendra seat for that flight. Once I got there to speak, I was honored by so much love they gave even from the poet. My cousin from Sarasota, FL even came to support. Spoken word is a part of a lifestyle, a relationship. So I'm not going anywhere. As far as Kendra and I, known as "Water," we got married two years later and had twins named Curtis and Constance. Those two CC's are my daily doses to keep moving forward from this point on. It's not all about me anymore and it never was actually, but through my kids I will always remain prominent in their lives no matter what. I built a foundation for them to stand on. So they too can stand on and be proud of who they are and maybe someday pass on this love.

Facing The Music

~Scene Fifteen~

Curtis Caliber Vanzant Jr

A year later my wife and I created a duet piece that shocked the world because it was televised. Including offers and talks of performing it from promoters at their venues to feature us in events.

{_= synchronized speaking}

Poet Tree

"A tree looks lonely>Apache

Without branches>Apache

And with no leaves>Water

It's dead>Water

<u>But leaves</u>

<u>Reminds me</u>

<u>Of the reflection of life</u>

<u>Through our kids</u>

<u>In this case family</u>

The roots grew>Apache

From the dirt>Apache

In which we originated>Water

Created a foundation>Apache

To stand on>Water

And in due time

Made a poetic rhythm

Where the

Designed structure

Is robust

Full of love and not lust

And trust

Is in God

To strengthen us

So this tree>Apache

Can remain intact>Apache

Never collapsing>Water

From high winds>Water

And lumber jacks>Water

<u>That attempt to</u>

<u>Bring down</u>

<u>What we build</u>

We make paper together>Apache

And still have our differences>Water

You damn right we do>Apache

You did not have to say that>Water

You didn't have to say that either>Apache

Look, do we have to get into this now>Water

Of course not>Apache

I love you>Apache

And I love you too">Water

A standing ovation was given for us. That piece made a difference in other people in their relationships. We both were interviewed after that. Stating that, our marriage could never be jeopardized by small problems and life's challenges. This example can even pertain to parents. The love that one would have should always be there even though they may disagree on certain things.

Significant others are different because they can be replaced, but devotion for another can be somewhat in the same. The wifey and I received Duet Of The Year for that piece. A great feeling and honor for the both of us.

As a result, you never know where life will take you sometimes. You just have to be ready for anything, even if that includes maintaining and being strong from things that you can't control. I was fortunate, if one would judge they would say I had it coming. Until you ask yourself. How would you have handled some of my situations? When it rains, you can be facing the music with two alternatives. You can either drown because of it, or grow from it. I chose to grow. Giving up is not an option in my book and neither should it be in yours. This may not be your average happy ending fairy tale, but this is his story, a poet's story.

Also check out:

It Gets Deeper Than Potholes: A Collection of Poems

www.amazon.com/dp/069235915X

www.createspacespace.com/5204256

www.ingramcontent.com/pod-product-compliance
Lightning Source LLC
LaVergne TN
LVHW091311080426
835510LV00007B/474